Hold My Cane!

LAUGH-OUT-LOUD BUCKET LIST ADVENTURES FOR THE YOUNG AT HEART

PLONKER PUBLISHING

Copyright © 2025 by Plonker Publishing

All rights reserved.

No portion of this book may be reproduced in any form without written permission from the publisher or author, except as permitted by U.S. copyright law.

Contents

Introduction	1
1. Grand Adventures	5
2. Culinary Conquests	15
3. Sentimental List	25
4. Tech Triumphs	33
5. Arts and Crafts	45
6. Comfortable Adventures	53
7. Brain Boosting	63
8. For The Soul	73
9. Oops! I Did it Again	83
10. Wild Card List	93
11. Your Legacy	103
12. Have A Laugh	111
13. Grandkids and Giggles	119
14. The Anti-Bucket List	129
15. Reflections on a Bucket Well-Listed	141

Introduction

Making a bucket list? Step one - remember where you put the bucket.

Congratulations! If you're reading this, you've already checked the first thing off your bucket list: "Open a book without falling asleep immediately." Well done, you overachiever, you!

Now, let's get one thing straight: this isn't your typical bucket list book. You won't find skydiving from a flaming helicopter into a shark-infested volcano on these pages—unless you've got some very enthusiastic insurance coverage. No, this book is about real adventures, genuine laughs, and moments you can enjoy without needing a chiropractor afterward.

Why a Bucket List? Why Now?

The idea of a bucket list isn't about squeezing every last drop out of life before you "kick the bucket," although, let's be honest, the phrase isn't exactly subtle. It's about finding joy in the little things, trying new experiences (or at least pretending to try them), and collecting stories you can tell your grandkids over and over... and over... until they've memorized every detail.

Life in your golden years isn't about slowing down; it's about slowing down strategically. It's about embracing every opportunity to laugh, learn, and live without worrying about looking cool. Because, let's face it, cool is overrated, and orthopedic shoes are fantastic.

What's This Book All About?

You'll find carefully crafted bucket list ideas tailored just for you inside these pages. From big adventures (like riding in a hot air balloon) to small triumphs (like finally mastering a Zoom call without accidentally turning yourself into a pink unicorn), every item is designed to be:

Fun: Yes, even the ones that involve vegetables.

Doable: No mountain climbing without a sherpa and oxygen tanks.

Memorable: Because what's life without a good story or two?

We've packed each chapter with practical tips, lighthearted humor, and just enough lousy advice to keep things interesting. Whether you're a go-getter ready to tackle the world or a couch conqueror mastering binge-watching, there's something here for you.

Who's This Book For?

This book is for you if:

You've **misplaced your glasses**... while they were on your head.

You've perfected the fine **art of the afternoon nap**.

You've said, "**Back in my day**..." at least once this week.

You believe that **age is just a number**—and yours comes with bonus wisdom points.

And hey, if you're a "young whippersnapper" reading this, congratulations on finding the perfect gift for your parents, grandparents, or that one neighbor who keeps shaking their fists at passing clouds.

Your Mission, Should You Choose to Accept It

This isn't a book you read cover-to-cover in one sitting (unless you're avoiding housework). It's a book you dip into whenever you feel adventurous or need a good chuckle. Keep it on your nightstand, coffee table, or next to the remote control (because, let's be honest, it's already there, isn't it?).

So grab your reading glasses, pour yourself a cup of tea (or something stronger—we won't judge), and get ready to start checking off some bucket list items. Remember, it's not about finishing the list; it's about enjoying every moment.

Ready? Take a deep breath (but not too deep—you might pull something), turn the page, and let's get started.

Let the bucket listing begin!

1

Grand Adventures

"Adventure" doesn't have to mean "Emergency Room Visit."

Congratulations, brave explorer! You've reached the first chapter, which means you're either genuinely excited to start your bucket list journey or you accidentally skipped ahead while adjusting your reading glasses. Regardless, you're here, and that's what matters.

Now, let's talk about adventure. When you hear the word, you might think of rugged explorers scaling mountains, brave souls swimming with sharks, or someone with excellent knees casually jumping out of an airplane. But let's be clear, you don't have to risk life and limb to have an adventure. In fact, most great adventures can be found a little closer to home. Preferably somewhere with padded seating and easy access to snacks.

This chapter is about embracing your adventure, which makes you smile, raises your heart rate just a little, and leaves you with a great story to tell your grandkids (or the cashier at the grocery store). So grab your sense of humor, a sturdy pair of walking shoes, and maybe some Tums. It's time to start ticking off your list!

Take a Hot Air Balloon Ride

(Soar Like a Bird, Scream Like a Human!)

There's something undeniably magical about floating gently above the earth in a **wicker basket powered by fire**. And yes, if you say it out loud like that, it does sound slightly insane. But here's the thing: hot air balloon rides are one of the safest, most peaceful adventures you can have. The world looks different from up there—quieter, softer, and surprisingly full of cows.

REALITY CHECK

The adventure starts early as balloons fly best at sunrise, so set your alarm (and prepare to question your **life choices at 5 a.m.**). Don't look down until you're **emotionally prepared**, because the ground suddenly looks much farther away when you're floating above it. If you happen to touch down in a random farmer's field, be ready to **apologize to a cow**—possibly multiple cows.

QUOTABLE

"I thought the most dangerous part would be the landing. Turns out, it was trying to gracefully climb into the basket without pulling a hamstring."

NO...SERIOUSLY?

Did you know that the first hot air balloon passengers in 1783 were a **sheep, a duck, and a rooster**? Scientists wanted to test if farm animals could handle high altitudes before sending up people. No word on whether the sheep tried to push anyone overboard.

And here's a fun fact: In some places, it's **traditional to gift a bottle of champagne** to the landowner if you accidentally crash-land in their field. Turns out, farmers are much more enthusiastic about uninvited balloons when free booze is involved.

GRAND ADVENTURE CHALLENGE 1

Go on a **hot air balloon ride**, take in the amazing view. **Bonus points** for shouting, "THERE'S A HOLE IN THE BALLOON!" at least once.

Climb a "Mountain"

(If You Can't Climb it, Point At it Dramatically)

Your "mountain" doesn't have to be Everest. It could be the modest hill in your local park, the slope leading to your neighbor's driveway, or, let's be honest, the slightly elevated speed bump at the grocery store. The goal is simple: get outside, breathe some fresh air, and enjoy that victorious feeling when you reach the top—or at least a nice bench halfway up.

REALITY CHECK

The **uphill journey** will have you questioning every life choice, from skipping leg day at the gym to that second slice of cake last night. The descent? That's when your **knees will remind you they are**, in fact, no longer 25. But hey, the view from the top (or middle) is bound to be at least somewhat worth it.

QUOTABLE

"I reached the peak of the highest hill in my neighborhood. It was 33 feet high. I celebrated with a selfie like I had just conquered Everest. Then I took the shortcut back down because my knees said, 'Absolutely not.'"

NO...SERIOUSLY?

Did you know the smallest official mountain in the world is **Mount Wycheproof** in Australia? It's a staggering 141 feet high. You could climb it in about 12 minutes, assuming you take a break for pictures and a dramatic wipe of your (imaginary) sweat.

And here's a fun fact: The first documented "mountain selfie" wasn't even a photo. It was a **sketch** drawn in 1853 by a British climber—because, well, cameras didn't exist yet. Now, that is dedication.

> ### GRAND ADVENTURE CHALLENGE 2
>
> **Find a nearby scenic spot** and take a moment to soak it in. Dramatically point into the distance.
> **Bonus points** if you do this in front of strangers who have no idea what's going on.

Dip Your Toes in an Ocean

(Sharks Not Invited)

Whether standing on the rocky shores of Maine or the sun-kissed beaches of Bali, there's something undeniably refreshing about dipping your toes into the ocean. The salty air, the cool water, and the tiny fish wondering why you're invading their space. It's pure magic.

REALITY CHECK

The **water will always be colder** than you expect. No exceptions. **Sand** will find its way into your belongings, your car, and possibly your soul. It's a lifelong commitment at this point. And someone, somewhere, will take a photo of you in your **"serene beach moment,"** only for it to look like you're being aggressively tackled by a rogue wave.

QUOTABLE

"I was ready for a tranquil moment by the sea. Instead, I got exfoliated by sand and mildly threatened by a seagull."

NO...SERIOUSLY?

Ever wonder why the ocean is so salty? Thank whales. A major contributor to the salt content? **Whale pee**. Thousands of gallons. Every day. Enjoy your swim.

And here's a fun thought: We've explored less than 5% of the ocean. That means there's a **95% chance** you're floating above something we don't even know exists. Sleep tight.

GRAND ADVENTURE CHALLENGE 3

Plan a beach day and stand in the waves. Don't think about what's lurking below the surface.
Bonus points if the seagulls don't steal your lunch.

Take a Cross-Country Train Trip

(Snacks are Mandatory)

Trains are the unsung heroes of travel. No cramped airplane seats, no terrifying turbulence, and no risk of being stuck next to someone trying to convince you of their obscure conspiracy theory. Instead, it's just you, a window view, and the soothing click-clack of the tracks.

REALITY CHECK

At some point, you will **make friends** with an overly chatty stranger; there's always one. Train food? An experience in itself. **Bring your own** like you're preparing for an impending apocalypse. And **train restrooms**? Let's just say they're an advanced-level challenge requiring balance, determination, and a strong sense of adventure.

QUOTABLE

"There's nothing quite like staring wistfully out a train window, pretending you're in an old-timey movie, while actually just looking at cows."

NO...SERIOUSLY?

The first train passengers were genuinely terrified that the human body couldn't handle speeds of **12 mph**. Fast forward to today, and high-speed trains can hit **374 mph**. Turns out, we adapted.

And here's a fun fact: The first dining car was invented because one wealthy man in the 1860s got **fed up with crumbs**. Tired of people dropping food in his lap on bumpy rides, he created a train restaurant. Priorities.

GRAND ADVENTURE CHALLENGE 4

Book a **scenic train trip**, pack plenty of snacks, and enjoy the rhythmic journey across landscapes. **Bonus points** if you wear one of those cool conductor hats.

Ride a Rollercoaster

(Choose The One With More Giggles Than Screams)

Rollercoasters aren't just for kids and adrenaline junkies. There's something exhilarating about a smooth, gentle ride that lets you feel alive... without questioning your life choices.

REALITY CHECK

Your official **ride photo** will be nothing short of **ridiculous**—accept it, frame it, and embrace the chaos. Even if the ride is mild, you'll **probably scream** at least once from excitement or sheer reflex. And let's be honest, cotton candy isn't just a fun treat; it's a well-earned reward for your bravery.

QUOTABLE

"I thought I was ready. The ride started, and suddenly, I was negotiating with a higher power to let me survive."

NO...SERIOUSLY?

Rollercoasters were originally designed as a **moral distraction**. In the 1880s, a businessman thought if people rode thrilling coasters, they'd stop wasting money on beer. Nope...didn't work.

And if you think your ride is fast, consider the **Formula Rossa in Abu Dhabi**, which reaches 149 mph in just 4.9 seconds—faster than most sports cars. Buckle up.

> **GRAND ADVENTURE CHALLENGE 5**
>
> Go to a **theme park**, pick the most "senior-friendly" rollercoaster, and enjoy the ride. Smile for the camera; you'll want proof.
> **Bonus points** if you don't scream.

Adventure Is All About Fun

Adventure doesn't always mean danger, speed, or altitude. Sometimes, it's about trying something new, l**aughing at yourself** when things don't go as planned, and collecting stories you'll tell again and again.

So pick one (or all) of these adventures, step out of your comfort zone (just a little), and remember: It's not about how fast you go but **how many snacks you bring**.

2

Culinary Conquests

Butter is your friend, and salad is a suggestion.

Welcome to the delicious chapter where we celebrate food—one bite, one laugh, and one slightly overcooked casserole at a time. Culinary adventures are about more than fine dining or Michelin stars. They're also about trying something new, laughing at the results, and eating dessert like it's your moral obligation.

Food is one of life's great pleasures, and at this stage, you've earned the right to eat whatever you want (within reason—no one wants to explain a churro-induced ER visit to the grandkids). So grab your favorite stretchy pants, fire up the oven (or just the microwave—no judgment), and let's dig in.

Eat Dessert First at a Fancy Restaurant

(Because Main Courses Are Just Speed Bumps To Sugar)

Who made the rule that dessert has to come last? Who decided you need to earn your cheesecake by chewing through a salad first? Let's flip the script. Order dessert first, savor every bite, and then decide if you still have room for vegetables. (Spoiler: you won't.)

REALITY CHECK

Smile confidently at the waiter; **dessert is not a crime**, it's a lifestyle choice. You might tell yourself dessert is enough, but let's be real, you'll probably **still order an entrée**. Your dining companion may judge you, or they **may join you** in sweet, rebellious solidarity.

QUOTABLE

"The waiter asked if I was sure I wanted cheesecake before my meal. I told him I'm a maverick eater with a higher purpose."

NO...SERIOUSLY?

In the U.S., **Casu Marzu**, a cheese filled with live maggots, is banned. But in Sardinia, it's considered a delicacy. Suddenly, your overpriced crème brûlée doesn't seem so bad.

And in 1976, a **giant blob of whipped cream** covered a town after a storage tank exploded. People thought it was the end of the world. Nope—just dessert.

CULINARY CONQUEST CHALLENGE 1

Go out to dinner and **start with dessert**—own your sweet-toothed rebellion.
Bonus points if you order two desserts and call it "research".

Create History with A Unique Recipe

(Yes, it Has To Be Edible)

Who says you must be a renowned chef to create a unique dish? Put together a recipe so unusual and awesome that it has never been done before. **Never. Before. In. Human. History**.

REALITY CHECK

Cook like **nobody's watching** because if they are, they might start questioning your choices. Your culinary masterpiece might resemble modern art... or something **scraped off the bottom of your oven**. And when it comes to tasting, let's just say **straws might need to be drawn.**

QUOTABLE

"We made an 'Arctic Banana Salad with Anchovies, M & M's and Mustard'. We didn't eat it. We just stared at it in awe."

NO...SERIOUSLY?

In 1938, a baker ran out of baker's chocolate, so she threw in broken chocolate pieces, expecting them to melt. Instead, she accidentally created the **first chocolate chip cookie**. Thank you, random kitchen disaster!

And if you think your recipe is ancient, consider this: the world's **oldest recipe** is a **4,000-year-old Mesopotamian stew** on a clay tablet. It included onions, meat, and beer—proving that ancient humans were just as food-obsessed as we are today.

CULINARY CONQUEST CHALLENGE 2

Create a dish that has never been done before, and revel in your culinary innovation.
Bonus points if you can keep it down.

Try a Dish You Can't Pronounce

(Eat First, Google Later)

Dining out is an adventure, especially when the menu looks like it's written in ancient hieroglyphics. But here's the thing: sometimes the best dishes are the ones you can't pronounce. Go on, order the Bouillabaisse or the Coq au Vin—even if it comes out as **"Boo-lee-baz"** and **"Cock-a-vain."**

REALITY CHECK

When in doubt, confidently point at the menu and say, "**That one, please**." Be prepared to use utensils you've never seen before—and **possibly struggle**. The dish might be a life-changing experience, or it might just be a **humbling lesson in culinary risk-taking**.

QUOTABLE

"I ordered something French. I think it was supposed to be chicken, but it has too many legs."

NO...SERIOUSLY?

Ordering in France? Be careful. Many tourists use "**preservatifs**" at a French restaurant, thinking it means preservatives. It actually means condoms. Awkward.

And if you think your meal smells a little strong, consider **Surströmming**, the Swedish delicacy of fermented herring. It's so pungent that some airlines ban it from being opened indoors. If food comes with a warning label, maybe rethink your choices.

CULINARY CONQUEST CHALLENGE 3

Go to an **international restaurant** and order the dish you can't pronounce.
Bonus points if you pretend to know precisely what it is.

Host a Wine and Cheese Night

(Grape Juice Counts)

There's something inherently **classy about hosting a wine and cheese night**. Even if your idea of fancy cheese is the kind that comes in individually wrapped slices, you can still set up a spread, pour some wine (or juice), and invite your most refined friends over. Or just your cat—no judgment

REALITY CHECK

Someone will absolutely **spill red wine** on something white. At least **one guest will pretend** to know what "full-bodied" means and nod thoughtfully while swirling their glass. And let's be honest, someone will **eat all the brie**. It might be you. It's definitely you.

QUOTABLE

"I swirled the wine, sniffed it, and said, 'Ah yes, notes of…grape.' I'm basically an expert now."

NO…SERIOUSLY?

The oldest wine ever found? Archaeologists discovered a **6,000-year-old jar of wine** in an ancient Armenian cave. No, they did not try to drink it (though you know someone wanted to).

And in 2021, bottles of **Bordeaux spent a year in space** as part of an experiment. The conclusion? It tasted… the same, but more expensive. Astronauts may be brilliant, but lack a decent wine palate.

CULINARY CONQUEST CHALLENGE 4

Host your own **wine and cheese night**. If you don't drink wine, make it a grape juice and crackers night.
Bonus points if you confidently make up a fake wine variety and convince others it's real.

Grow Your Own Vegetables

(Start With Something Resilient. Like Weeds)

There's something magical about eating food you've grown yourself. But let's face it, **not everyone was born with a green thumb**. If your past gardening attempts have ended in tragedy, don't worry—basil is forgiving (unlike that tomato plant you forgot to water for three weeks).

REALITY CHECK

Something will eat your tomatoes before you do. Probably a squirrel. You will **overwater or underwater** your plants at least once. It's part of the process. And that first harvest? It will taste like victory... and maybe a **little bit of dirt**.

QUOTABLE

"I grew three cherry tomatoes this year. I'm practically a farmer now. I think I'm gonna buy a cow next."

NO...SERIOUSLY?

Plants can actually "**talk**" to each other. Studies show that some plants warn others of danger by releasing chemicals into the air. That tomato plant? It's probably gossiping about you.

And if you think gardening is challenging, try doing it in space. Astronauts have grown **lettuce, radishes, and mustard greens** in zero gravity. Because even in space, you still need your greens.

CULINARY CONQUEST CHALLENGE 5

Plant something—anything—and try to keep it alive.
Bonus points if it lasts a month.

Food Is About More Than Eating

Food is about connection, laughter, and sometimes a little bit of **culinary chaos**. Whether ordering dessert first, experimenting with an unpronounceable dish, or hosting the fanciest cheese night known to mankind, every bite is a chance for a mini adventure.

So put on your best elastic waistband pants, grab a fork, and remember: **Calories don't count if you're having fun**.

3

Sentimental List

MEMORIES ARE THE BEST SOUVENIRS—AND SO ARE FRIDGE MAGNETS.

Welcome to the chapter that makes you laugh, makes you cry, and will make you pause and reflect. While some bucket list adventures are about excitement and adrenaline, others are about connection, legacy, and leaving behind stories worth telling.

This isn't about being overly sappy (though a tear or two is totally allowed). It's about taking a moment to appreciate the people you love, the stories you've collected, and the footprints you're leaving behind—preferably ones in soft sand and not in wet cement.

So grab a warm cup of something comforting, and let's dive into the sentimental side of your bucket list. Warning: this chapter pairs well with cozy blankets and nostalgic playlists.

Write Letters to People You Care About

(A letter Is Just a Hug On Paper)

When was the last time you **wrote an actual letter** to someone. Not an email, not a text, but an honest-to-goodness letter on paper, with your handwriting and maybe even a doodle in the corner. Letters are time capsules of love, gratitude, and sometimes hilariously bad penmanship.

REALITY CHECK

Write from the **heart, not the head.** Your first draft might **sound awkward.** Keep going. People will **treasure your letter** more than you realize.

QUOTABLE

"I wrote a heartfelt letter to my grandkids. They texted back, 'What's this weird paper thing?'"

NO...SERIOUSLY?

The **world's oldest love letter** was written on a 4,000-year-old clay tablet from ancient Mesopotamia. Apparently, romance has always been complicated.

And in the 1800s, people **paid for letters** based on the **number of words.** Stamps were so expensive that people wrote in microscopic handwriting to fit as much as possible.

SENTIMENTAL CHALLENGE 1

Write a letter to someone important in your life. Tell them something meaningful.
Bonus Points if they write back.

Share a Family Recipe

(Write it Down. If Unsure, Make Up The Ingredients. Add a Disclaimer, Just in Case)

Food has a **magical way of connecting people** across generations. Whether it's Grandma's secret cookie recipe, Dad's famous barbecue sauce, or your own special "Midnight Snack Surprise," these recipes deserve to be shared, written down, and passed along.

REALITY CHECK

Someone will **mess up your recipe.** They'll still love it. Someone will claim **their version tastes better.** Most importantly, the recipe will live on long after the **cook has retired**.

QUOTABLE

"Step 7: Stir casually while pretending you're on a cooking show. Optional: Wear an apron that says, 'Kiss the Cook.'"

NO...SERIOUSLY?

Some family recipes are literally secret. KFC's **11 herbs and spices** are so top-secret that only two people know the full recipe, and it's locked in a vault.

And in the ultimate power move, a grandma **once went viral** for guarding her recipe. She refused to share her famous cookies, so her obituary simply said, "Sorry, you'll never get it now."

> ### SENTIMENTAL CHALLENGE 2
>
> Write down your **favorite family recipe.** Cook it with someone special.
> **Bonus Points** if you leave cryptic notes in the margins.

Create a Photo Album

(Every Photo Has a Story. Don't Include That One Where You Pooped Your Pants At The Prom)

We all have that **box (or folder on our phone)** overflowing with photos. Some are blurry, some are accidental selfies, and some are pure gold. Turning those moments into a physical or digital album is like building a treasure chest of memories.

REALITY CHECK

You'll spend **hours reminiscing** instead of organizing. You'll probably **laugh at hairstyles from the '80s.** And some photos might need to be **"accidentally" left out** of the album.

QUOTABLE

"I tried to make a photo album. I spent an hour staring at one photo of me holding a fish in 1974. It was a good fish."

NO...SERIOUSLY?

In the **1800s,** people used to **pose with their deceased relatives** for final family photos, because creepy traditions are timeless.

Photographer **Noah Kalina** started taking **daily selfies in 2000.** Now we can watch him age in 5 minutes.

SENTIMENTAL CHALLENGE 3

Start a **photo album.** Pick 10-20 of your favorite photos and arrange them.
Bonus Points if you add funny captions.

Tell Your Favorite Life Story

(Every Good Story Needs a Dramatic............. Pause............
So Use It Wisely)

Everyone has that one story—the one you've told a dozen times, but it still gets a laugh (or a gasp) every time. Maybe it's about when you got lost in a foreign country, that one birthday party disaster, or how you met your best friend. Share it. Loudly. Dramatically. With all the flair you can muster.

REALITY CHECK

Your audience might **already know the ending.** Tell it anyway. **Exaggeration is allowed.** Encouraged, even. Your grandkids will roll their eyes but secretly **love it.**

QUOTABLE

"I started telling my favorite story, and halfway through realized I'd already told it last week. Then I got flustered and forgot the end. Nobody noticed."

NO...SERIOUSLY?

Storytelling can lower stress. Studies show that telling personal stories reduces anxiety and boosts happiness—so yes, Grandpa's fishing stories are technically therapy.

Your **brain loves stories more than facts**. People remember stories 22 times better than plain facts. So, that's why you remember your embarrassing childhood moments forever.

> **SENTIMENTAL CHALLENGE 4**
>
> **Gather an audience** (even if it's just the goldfish) and tell your favorite life story with gusto.
> **Bonus Points** if there's more than one human in the audience.

The Little Things Are the Big Things

The sentimental side of your bucket list isn't about grand gestures but small, **meaningful moments** that create lasting ripples. Whether you write a letter, tell a story, or pass on a recipe, every little action becomes part of your legacy.

So share, laugh, cry a little if you need to, and know this: Your story matters, and **someone will treasure every word**.

4

Tech Triumphs

Siri thinks you're talking to someone named "Cereal."

Ah, technology. It's everywhere. Phones, tablets, smartwatches, doorbells that talk to you—it's like living in a science fiction movie, but with worse tech support. If you've ever tried to send a text, accidentally activated your flashlight, or spent ten minutes yelling "HELLO? HELLO?" on a Zoom call while muted, this chapter is for you.

But here's the thing: technology isn't the enemy. It's just… stubborn, like a toaster that occasionally sets off the smoke alarm but still makes decent toast. And whether you're trying to FaceTime your grandkids, order groceries online, or simply figure out where the heck your photos went, you can do this.

Welcome to Tech Triumphs, where the buttons are tiny, the Wi-Fi is temperamental, and autocorrect is your nemesis.

Master the Art of Texting

(Use Your Thumb. Your Finger is For Pointing)

Texting is supposed to make communication faster. So why does it feel like it takes 45 minutes to type "See you soon"? Between tiny keyboards, autocorrect disasters, and your phone deciding it's smarter than you, it's a wonder anyone communicates.

REALITY CHECK

Autocorrect is your greatest enemy. It will betray you at least once a week, probably in a way that makes you question your life choices. **Your thumb will cramp** from typing, but no, you cannot count it as a workout. **And emojis? They're not hieroglyphics**…you don't have to use all of them at once.

QUOTABLE

"I typed 'Let's meet at noon,' but autocorrect sent 'Let's meat at moon.' Now I'm worried they'll actually show up with steak at midnight."

NO…SERIOUSLY?

The first **SMS text message** ever sent in 1992 simply said, "Merry Christmas." No emojis, no typos—just festive simplicity.

And if you think you text a lot, consider this: The average person sends **94 texts a day**, which adds up to more than 2 million keystrokes per year. Who needs the gym when you've got thumb cardio?

TECH TRIUMPHS CHALLENGE 1

Send a **text message** with no typos, emojis, or autocorrect disasters.
Bonus points if the recipient understands it first time.

Take a Selfie

(Stop Looking For The Selfie Button on The Back of The Phone. Honestly, There's No Button)

Selfies are supposed to be fun, casual snapshots of your face. But let's be honest—getting a good selfie is more complicated than it looks. Your camera's in reverse mode, your forehead takes up 80% of the screen, and somehow, the flash is on. But here's the thing: selfies are a modern art form, and you're about to become Picasso.

REALITY CHECK

Your first selfie attempt will look like a **crime scene photo**; accept it and move on. Lighting is **everything** (and no, standing next to a lamp doesn't count). And **smiling naturally while holding a phone** in front of your face? Harder than it sounds

QUOTABLE

"Attempted a group selfie, but my arm's too short, so now it's just everyone else and half my forehead."

NO...SERIOUSLY?

A **curious monkey** once stole a photographer's camera, who then snapped a perfect selfie. A legal battle followed over who owned the rights: the monkey or the photographer.

And here's a wild fact—more people have **died taking selfies** in risky locations than from shark attacks. Maybe step away from the edge of that cliff, dude.

> ### TECH TRIUMPHS CHALLENGE 2
>
> **Take a selfie** that you're proud of. No ceiling fan, no double chin, and no blurry finger over the camera lens. **Bonus points** if you get it right on the first try.

Lost And Found with Satellite Navigation

(Maps Are For Amateurs)

You're about to enter the future of navigation. With satellite navigation (GPS), you'll never get lost again—unless your phone decides you'd rather take a scenic route to the grocery store. Welcome to the world where every turn is dictated by a tiny voice in your phone that thinks it knows you better than you do.

REALITY CHECK

Your GPS will lead you down roads you **didn't even know existed**. Traffic rerouting will make you question whether your phone is helping or **trolling you**. And that "**shortcut**" it suggests? Yeah, you're probably going to need snacks.

QUOTABLE

"I followed the GPS into a parking lot. I think it just needed to rest for a while."

NO...SERIOUSLY?

A tourist in Iceland once **blindly followed GPS directions** onto a closed road, got stuck, and was fined for trespassing. The moral of the story: don't trust your phone over road signs.

And here's an interesting fact—GPS satellites adjust their clocks daily because time moves slightly faster in space due to relativity. So technically, your **GPS knows the future... by milliseconds.**

TECH TRIUMPHS CHALLENGE 3

Use **satellite navigation** to get to a new destination. **Bonus points** if you eventually arrive with your sanity still intact.

Host a Zoom Call

(The Mute Button is Your Friend. Also, Your Greatest Enemy)

Zoom calls are a **miracle of modern technology**. You can talk to family across the country, attend virtual book clubs, or accidentally join a meeting while still wearing pajamas.

REALITY CHECK

Your camera will always catch you from the **least flattering** angle possible. The **mute button will win every argument**, often without your knowledge. And let's be honest, someone will shout, "**Can you hear me now**?" at least five times before the meeting really starts.

QUOTABLE

"I thought I nailed my Zoom call today. Then I realized I'd been talking to myself for ten minutes. The mute button strikes again."

NO...SERIOUSLY?

A lawyer in a virtual court hearing once got **stuck as a talking cat filter** and had to convince the judge, "I'm not a cat, Your Honor."

In 2020, astronauts aboard the International Space Station joined a Zoom call from orbit—proving that **even astronauts can't escape virtual meetings**.

TECH TRIUMPHS CHALLENGE 4

Successfully **host or join a Zoom call** without tech glitches.
Bonus points if you look confident doing it.

Set a Password You'll Actually Remember

(No, "ArnoldSchwarzenegger." is Not a Strong Password)

Ah, passwords—the **gatekeepers of the digital world**. Theoretically, they protect your accounts from hackers. In reality, they mainly protect you from… yourself. Because who can remember **Tr0ub@dor!92#** without writing it on a sticky note taped to their computer screen?

REALITY CHECK

Every website has different rules. One demands an uppercase letter, another insists on a symbol, and one might as well require a **blood sample**. At some point, you will **lock yourself out** of your own account. Password managers exist, but trusting them feels like letting a **robot hold your wallet**.

QUOTABLE

"My password is so secure, even I can't figure it out. It's like I've hacked myself."

NO...SERIOUSLY?

In 2019, **NASA was hacked** because someone used a weak, guessable password. So yes, even rocket scientists get lazy.

And if you think your hiding spots are genius, studies show people stash passwords in books, under keyboards, and even inside sock drawers. Because sure, **hackers never check socks**.

TECH TRIUMPHS CHALLENGE 5

Create **one strong password** and actually remember it.
Write it down somewhere safe-ish.
Bonus points if, in a week, you remember where you wrote it down.

Learn How to Use YouTube

(Set a Timer. Trust Me On This One)

YouTube is a treasure trove of knowledge, entertainment, and people doing really questionable things with watermelons. But it's also a **black hole**. You start watching a video on how to fix your sink, and suddenly it's 2 AM, and you're watching a guy build a log cabin with a spoon.

REALITY CHECK

One video leads to **300** more. At some point, you will watch at least one **cat video**—it's unavoidable. And just when you're fully engaged, ads will show up **every 30 seconds** to remind you why patience is a virtue.

QUOTABLE

"I went on YouTube to learn how to fix my leaky faucet. Four hours later, I was watching penguins dance to disco music. Good dancers, those penguins."

NO...SERIOUSLY?

The first **YouTube upload** in 2005 was called "Me at the Zoo," featuring a guy standing in front of elephants. That's it.

No viral dance moves, no drama, just pure, unfiltered early internet magic.

And if you ever doubt humanity's priorities, remember this: The most-viewed video ever is **Baby Shark,** with over 13 billion views. That's more than the population of Earth. We are doomed.

TECH TRIUMPHS CHALLENGE 6

Watch one YouTube instructional video and follow through with what it teaches you
Bonus points if you manage to avoid the cat videos.

Conquer the Tech, Own the Day

Technology isn't here to make your life harder, though it feels that way sometimes. But with **patience, a lot of humor, and maybe one grandchild** on speed dial for emergencies, you'll master texting, selfies, Zoom calls, and YouTube like a pro.

Remember: every mistake is just a learning opportunity. And **every autocorrect fail is just free comedy material**.

5

Arts and Crafts

Coloring Outside the Lines Is a Lifestyle Choice.

Welcome to the chapter where creativity knows no age limits and glue sticks are a valid life choice. Whether you were born with the soul of an artist or the fine motor skills of a sleep-deprived octopus, this chapter is your chance to create something amazing (or at least something... recognizable).

Arts and crafts are about creating masterpieces, having fun, expressing yourself, and maybe getting messy along the way. So roll up your sleeves, put on your least favorite shirt (glue and glitter have a vendetta against clothing), and let's get crafting!

There's no such thing as a craft failure, just an abstract success story.

Paint Something...Anything

(Slap Some Paint On it And Call it Inspired)

You don't need to be Monet or Van Gogh to enjoy painting. In fact, the messier, the better! Whether it's a canvas, a rock, a piece of wood, or that one wall in your house you've been meaning to repaint for five years, this is your moment to embrace your inner artist.

REALITY CHECK

Your masterpiece may look more like a toddler's **finger** painting than the Sistine Chapel—just call it modern art. Paint has a magical way of appearing in unexpected places: your **elbow, your hair, and somehow... your socks**? Mixing colors is exciting—until everything mysteriously turns into seven **shades of brown**.

QUOTABLE

"I tried to paint a sunset. Somehow, it turned into a cross-eyed potato."

NO...SERIOUSLY?

Bob Ross's **famous perm** was actually an accident. He hated his signature curly hair but kept it because it became his brand. Essentially, he was stuck with "happy little curls" forever.

And here's a fun fact: The **Mona Lisa has no eyebrows.** Art historians believe Leonardo da Vinci either never finished painting them or simply faded over time. Either way, she's totally rocking the no-brow look.

ARTS & CRAFTS CHALLENGE 1

Paint something—anything. A canvas, a wall, or even a rock. Frame it and display it proudly.
Bonus points if you leave that paint on your nose for a few days.

Write a Poem

(No, it Doesn't Have to Rhyme)

Poetry isn't just for brooding teenagers with leather journals. It's for anyone with **something to say**, or even just **something to laugh** about. Write about love and life, the time you lost your keys, or how your cat judges you silently from across the room.

REALITY CHECK

Your first draft might sound like a grocery list, but that's okay. Rhyming is **hard**. Like a **yard**. Or a piece of **cake**... see what I mean? If you're stuck, just start with "**Roses are red**..." and see where it takes you.

QUOTABLE

"I made my family listen to my poem. Only the dog stayed awake."

NO...SERIOUSLY?

The famous "**Roses are red, violets are blue**..." is really old—the first recorded version dates back to 1590, meaning people have been writing cheesy love poems for over 400 years.

And did you know? Dr. Seuss wrote **Green Eggs and Ham** on a dare. His publisher bet him he couldn't write a book using 50 words or less. He did—and it sold over 200 million copies.

ARTS & CRAFTS CHALLENGE 2

Write a poem. Funny, serious, or completely nonsensical—it doesn't matter.
Bonus points if you perform it dramatically for someone.

Crochet and Conquer the Yarn Monster

(Start Small. Like... Really Small. Maybe a Coaster)

Knitting and crocheting aren't just for **grandmas in rocking chairs**. They're for cool grandmas in rocking chairs. And cool grandpas. And honestly, anyone with patience and the ability to untangle yarn without breaking down emotionally.

REALITY CHECK

Your first scarf will **probably** look more like a potholder. Dropped stitches? **A rite of passage**. And if you have a cat, **prepare for chaos**. Yarn and feline curiosity do not mix well.

QUOTABLE

"I dropped my knitting needle and now my dog thinks we're playing fetch."

NO...SERIOUSLY?

Napoleon banned knitting needles because he believed spies were hiding secret messages in knitted scarves. Strange guy, that Napoleon.

And...knitting used to be a **male-only profession**. In the 16th century, knitting guilds only allowed men because it was considered a serious trade. Today, your grandma is showing them how it's done.

> ### ARTS & CRAFTS CHALLENGE 3
>
> **Knit or crochet something**—a scarf, a potholder, or just a gloriously tangled mess you can call "yarn sculpture."
> **Bonus points** if someone actually recognizes what it is.

Start Your Memoir

(Start With The Fun Stories That Make People Laugh)

Everyone has stories worth telling. Whether you stormed the beaches of *Normandy* or survived the horrors of dial-up internet, your life is packed with tales that deserve to be shared.

REALITY CHECK

Writing about your life **might stir up unexpected emotions**—and that's okay. You'll remember tiny details from **40 years** ago but forget what you had for **breakfast**. And let's be honest, you might get **distracted for three hours** organizing old photos instead of writing.

QUOTABLE

"I started writing my memoir. So far, I've written the title and my name and stared dramatically out the window for two hours. It's easier than I thought".

NO...SERIOUSLY?

Benjamin Franklin wrote his memoir in the third person. Apparently, he wanted to sound more important, so he wrote his entire autobiography like he was talking about someone else.

And get this—the oldest known memoir is over **1,800 years old**. It was written by a Roman Emperor (who happened to be Julius Caesar's nephew). His main theme? How awesome he was.

ARTS & CRAFTS CHALLENGE 4

Write one story from your life. It doesn't have to be long or perfect—just honest.
Bonus points if you use the word "pirate" at least once.

Creativity Is About Joy, Not Perfection

Arts and crafts aren't about skill, they're about expression, fun, and **not taking yourself too seriously**. Whether you're painting a masterpiece, writing your life story, or knitting a wonky scarf, every creative moment is a victory.

So grab your paintbrush, yarn, or glitter (just... be careful with the glitter), and dip your toes in. And remember: art isn't about being perfect—**it's about enjoying the mess**.

6

Comfortable Adventures

Sometimes, the best adventures happen in pajamas.

Welcome to the chapter where adventure meets comfort. You only need a cozy blanket, your favorite snacks, and possibly a TV remote with batteries that work. Who said adventure involves hiking boots, packed suitcases, or leaving the house?

Some of the best stories, exciting discoveries, and biggest laughs happen right from the comfort of your home—preferably while wearing elastic-waist pants and sipping something warm (or something with a little kick; we don't judge).

So fluff up your cushions, adjust your recliner to the "perfectly lazy" position, and prepare for adventures that don't require sunscreen, bug spray, or shoes.

Master the Mini-Snooze

(Wake Refreshed, Not Confused)

Napping is a skill, and like any skill, it requires practice. A good power nap can refresh your brain, recharge your energy, and make you feel like you've discovered the secrets of the universe. But beware: cross the line into "accidental marathon nap" territory, and you'll wake up wondering what year it is.

REALITY CHECK

Finding the perfect **nap duration** is an art form. **Set an alarm**—don't let that power nap become a full-blown hibernation. And let's be honest, a **post-nap snack is practically mandatory.**

QUOTABLE

"I said I'd nap for 20 minutes. I woke up two hours later with the cat on my head and no idea what day it was."

NO...SERIOUSLY?

Naps make you smarter. A 20-minute nap improves memory, creativity, and learning ability. So technically, falling asleep at your desk is just "brain training."

And if you think you're tired, consider this: **The Guinness World Record** for staying awake is 11 days straight in 1964 by a student. He then promptly slept for 14 hours.

> ### COMFORTABLE ADVENTURES CHALLENGE 1
>
> **Master the 20-minute power nap**. Find the perfect cozy spot, set your alarm, and commit to a proper session.
> **Bonus points** if you don't drool.

Conquer a Book in a Day

(Picture Books Don't Count)

Books are portals to other worlds. The great thing about them is you can visit those worlds without ever getting out of your chair. It could be an epic fantasy, a heartwarming memoir, or a mystery novel that keeps you guessing, there's something magical about getting lost in a good book for hours.

REALITY CHECK

Your eyes will start to cross around **hour three**. You'll probably need **more** refreshments than anticipated. And at some point, you'll look at the clock and wonder **where the day went**.

QUOTABLE

"I read the whole book in 12 hours, and now I'm recommending it to everyone like it's my life's mission."

NO...SERIOUSLY?

The fastest reader ever is **Howard Berg**, who can read 25,000 words per minute. At that speed, he could finish an entire Harry Potter book in under 15 minutes.

And if you think you can finish the longest novel ever written in a day, think again. **À la recherche du temps perdu** (*In Search of Lost Time*) by *Marcel Proust* is over 1.2 million words long. You'd need more than one day (or a time machine).

COMFORTABLE ADVENTURES CHALLENGE 2

Spend an entire day **reading a book** from start to finish. **Bonus points** if it's a book you've meant to read for years.

Watch an Entire TV Series

(Snacks Within Arm's Reach are Non-Negotiable)

There's a certain kind of **heroism** in watching an **entire TV series** in one sitting. Whether it's a crime thriller, a tear-jerking drama, or a cooking competition show that makes you question your life choices (Why didn't I become a pastry chef?), binge-watching is a modern-day quest.

REALITY CHECK

Your neck will hurt from looking at the screen for **14 hours** straight. You'll start talking to the characters like they're your **real-life friends**. And let's be honest, you'll definitely say, "**Just one more episode**..." at least eight times.

QUOTABLE

"I watched an entire season in one day. I feel both accomplished and slightly ashamed. But mostly accomplished."

NO...SERIOUSLY?

Binge-watching can actually **change your brain**. Watching TV for too long tricks your mind into thinking you're experiencing the events, which is why we get so emotionally attached to fictional characters.

And fun fact—the first regular TV show was **The Queen's Messenger**, aired in 1928. It had two viewers.

> **COMFORTABLE ADVENTURES CHALLENGE 3**
>
> Pick a series you've always wanted to watch and **binge it unapologetically**.
> **Bonus points** if you stay awake the whole time.

Host a Virtual Game Night

(Choose Games That Won't End in Family Feuds)

Virtual game nights are one of the **greatest gifts of the digital age**. You can laugh, play, and trash-talk your friends without leaving your couch. It might be online trivia, virtual charades, or a digital board game. The goal is simple: have fun, stay connected, and try not to let Aunt Linda win again.

REALITY CHECK

Someone will have tech issues. It's practically a rule. Competitive relatives will **reveal themselves** braced for impact. And, inevitably, someone will **spill a drink** on their keyboard.

QUOTABLE

"We played online Pictionary. My drawing of a chicken looked like a confused walrus with wings."

NO...SERIOUSLY?

Some people **cheat at virtual board games**. A study found that 33% of players admit to secretly cheating in games like online Monopoly. That's low, people.

The first online game was in 1978. It was called MUD (*Multi-User Dungeon*) and basically Dungeons & Dragons, but text-based. The internet has come a long way.

COMFORTABLE ADVENTURES CHALLENGE 4

Host or join a **virtual game night**. Pick a game that encourages laughter, creativity, and friendly competition.
Bonus points if you actually win a round.

Watch the Sunrise Or Sunset

(Bring a Warm Drink and a Cozy Blanket)

When was the last time you just sat and **watched the sun rise or set** without distraction, without scrolling through your phone, and without mentally planning your grocery list? The world slows down during these moments, and you might just find yourself feeling a little more… peaceful.

REALITY CHECK

It'll feel cold. Bring layers. **Nature is loud** at sunrise. Birds have zero chill. But trust us—it's **worth every minute**.

QUOTABLE

"I watched the sunrise this morning. I felt peaceful, reflective… and sleepy…forgot my coffee."

NO…SERIOUSLY?

The earth's atmosphere **makes the sun late**. The sun actually rises a few minutes before it "looks like" it does because the atmosphere bends the light. So, technically, you're watching an optical illusion.

And if you think you're dedicated, there's a group of travelers called "**Sunset Chasers**" who fly to different countries just to catch the best sunsets.

COMFORTABLE ADVENTURES CHALLENGE 5

Wake up early to **catch the sunrise** or carve out time to watch the sunset. No distractions allowed.
Bonus Points for doing it with company.

Comfort Is the New Adventure

Not every adventure needs hiking boots, plane tickets, or sunscreen. **Some of the best moments happen right at home**, with good snacks, cozy blankets, and Wi-Fi that (hopefully) doesn't cut out halfway through your favorite show.

Whether binge-watching a series, planning a dream vacation from your recliner, or finally mastering the ancient art of napping, these comfortable adventures are just as meaningful as any mountain top sunrise.

So lean back, fluff your pillows, and remember: **Adventure is a state of mind**—and elastic pants are always a good idea.

7

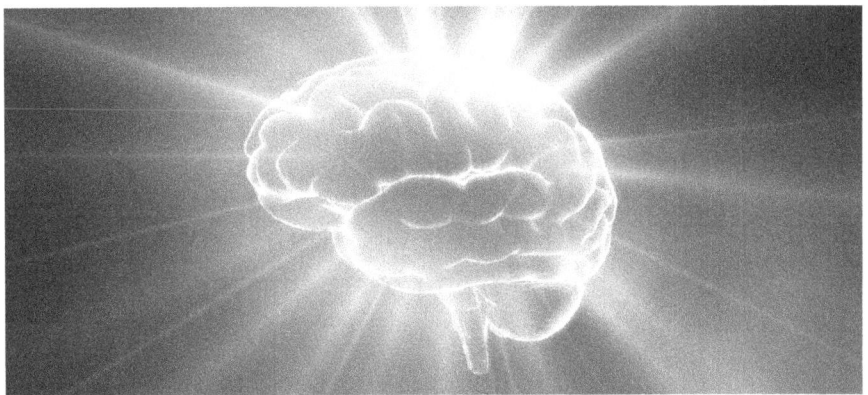

Brain Boosting

Finding your glasses doesn't count.

Ah, the brain is a marvel of human engineering, capable of storing decades of memories, solving complex problems, and remembering every lyric to songs from 1977. Yet, it occasionally struggles to recall where you left your glasses (spoiler: they're probably on your head).

But here's the good news: just like your muscles, your brain can get stronger with a bit of exercise. No, not squats and push-ups (thank goodness)—we're talking puzzles, trivia, creative thinking, and perhaps a little detective work.

So sharpen your metaphorical pencils, grab a cup of tea (or something stronger—we're not judging), and let's give your brain the attention it deserves.

Conquer a Crossword Puzzle

(Cheat a Little, Celebrate a Lot)

Crosswords are like the **gym workouts of the word world**. They challenge your memory, improve your vocabulary, and occasionally remind you of long-forgotten trivia (*like the capital of Kyrgyzstan or Tom Cruise's second wife*).

REALITY CHECK

You will stare at one clue for **20 minutes** and then suddenly solve it while **brushing your teeth later**. Some crossword creators have a twisted sense of humor. And remember, **it's not cheating if you call it "research."**

QUOTABLE

"The crossword clue said 'common fruit,' and my brain decided to forget every fruit."

NO...SERIOUSLY?

During **WWII**, a British officer banned his troops from crosswords because they were too distracted to train for battle. Priorities, people.

And if you think you're fast, consider this: The **quickest crossword champions** can complete a New York Times puzzle in under two minutes. The rest of us just stare at 3 Across for an hour.

> ### BRAIN BOOSTING CHALLENGE 1
>
> **Complete an entire crossword puzzle**. We'll allow it if you must peek at a clue or two.
> **Bonus points** if it's one you haven't done before.

Start a Daily Journal

(Like Therapy, But Cheaper)

Journaling is about keeping your **brain active and reflective**. One day, your grandkids might find it and think, "Wow, Grandma was hilarious!"

REALITY CHECK

Your handwriting might make it look like you wrote it **underwater**. Your words will **mean more to someone someday** than you'll ever know. And remember, it's not about being **profound**—it's about being you.

QUOTABLE

"Day 1: Started a journal. Day 2: Forgot to write in the journal. Day 3: Lost the journal. Day 4: Started a journal."

NO...SERIOUSLY?

Journaling can **help you sleep**. Writing down thoughts before bed reduces stress and improves sleep. So basically, your diary is better than melatonin.

And here's a fun fact: **Leonardo da Vinci wrote backward** in his notebooks so they could only be read in a mirror. A bit weird that da Vinci dude.

BRAIN BOOSTING CHALLENGE 2

Start a brain journal. Write something—anything—once a day for a week.
Bonus points if you don't lose the journal.

Learn a New Phrase in a Foreign Language

(Start With Something Useful, Like "Where's The Bathroom?" or "More Beer, Please")

Learning a new language **keeps your brain sharp**, builds your confidence, and can make you feel incredibly accomplished. You don't need to become fluent; just knowing a few phrases can add some flair to your next vacation… or your next visit to the international foods aisle.

REALITY CHECK

Pronunciation is **more complicated than it looks**. You'll probably sound like an overly confident tourist. And yes, Google Translate is your new best friend.

QUOTABLE

"I tried learning French. I can now confidently ask the waiter for a lampshade with fries."

NO…SERIOUSLY?

The Japanese have a word for a useless person. **Bakkushan** means someone who looks attractive… until you see them from the front. Brutal.

Some words have no English equivalent. The German word **Kummerspeck** means "grief bacon"—the weight you gain from stress eating. Yes, we need this word in English.

BRAIN BOOSTING CHALLENGE 3

Learn **at least one phrase** in a foreign language. Use it on someone, even if it's your dog.
Bonus points if it is in Klingon.

Play a Brain-Boosting Game

(Start With Something Fun Like Sudoku, Trivia, or a Good Old-Fashioned Jigsaw Puzzle)

Brain games are everywhere. On your phone, in newspapers, and even on those cereal boxes you used to read as a kid. The key is to have fun while secretly giving your brain a mental push-up.

REALITY CHECK

Sudoku will make you question your **life choices**. Trivia questions will remind you how much **random knowledge you don't have**. And your **competitive streak** might surprise even you.

QUOTABLE

"The app said, 'Great job!' after I failed. Even my phone's pitying me now."

NO...SERIOUSLY?

Chess used to be a crime. In 1254, King Louis IX of France banned chess, calling it a distraction from war. Ironically, chess is literally a war game.

And get this—**playing video games improves memory**. Studies show that Tetris can reduce stress and even help prevent PTSD. So, playing for hours? It's science

---

BRAIN BOOSTING CHALLENGE 4

Play a **brain-boosting game** like Sudoku or Trivia.
Bonus points if you cheat only a little.

Solve a Mystery

(Start Small. Like Missing Socks. Or Black Holes)

Mysteries aren't just for **Sherlock Holmes**; they're for anyone with a curious mind and a slightly suspicious outlook on life. Whether it's a murder mystery novel, an online escape room, or just figuring out why the remote is always missing, solving puzzles keeps your mind sharp.

REALITY CHECK

Mystery books will keep you **awake past your bedtime**. Escape rooms (even virtual ones) will make you question your **problem-solving** skills. And sometimes, the **sock thief is**... **your neighbor's dog**.

QUOTABLE

"I solved the mystery of 'Who ate the last cookie?' It was yummy."

NO...SERIOUSLY?

Sherlock Holmes never said, "Elementary, My Dear Watson." It never appears in any Sherlock Holmes book—it was made up by movie adaptations.

Think your puzzles take time? Consider this: The **Zodiac Killer's** code took 51 years to solve. A team of amateur codebreakers finally cracked the message in 2020.

> ### BRAIN BOOSTING CHALLENGE 5
>
> Read a **mystery novel** or try an escape room game (virtual or in-person).
> **Bonus points** if you solve it without cheating.

Memorize a Joke and Tell It Perfectly

(Practice in Front Of a Mirror or Your Favorite Houseplant)

Telling a joke is an **art form**. The setup, the delivery, the pause before the punchline—it's all carefully orchestrated. And when you nail it? Pure comedy gold.

REALITY CHECK

Laughter is contagious. Scientists found that just hearing laughter activates the part of your brain that makes you want to laugh too. So, reading jokes? Basically brain exercise.

QUOTABLE

"I told a joke at dinner. Nobody laughed, but I'm pretty sure they were just stunned by my genius."

NO...SERIOUSLY?

Laughter is contagious. Scientists found that just hearing laughter activates the part of your brain that makes you want to laugh too. So, reading jokes? Basically brain exercise.

The oldest joke in the world is from 1900 BC: *"Something which has never occurred since time immemorial: A young woman did not fart in her husband's lap."* Yep, fart jokes...timeless.

BRAIN BOOSTING CHALLENGE 6

Memorize one **great joke** and tell it flawlessly. Preferably at a family dinner or in a Zoom call where people can't walk away.
Bonus points if no one groans.

Your Brain Deserves a Victory Lap

Your brain is a powerhouse, and it deserves some love and attention. Whether you're conquering crosswords, mastering a foreign phrase, or solving the world's smallest mysteries, every little brain-boosting activity counts.

So keep puzzling, keep learning, and most importantly, **keep laughing**. Because a brain filled with curiosity and humor is a brain that stays sharp.

8

FOR THE SOUL

SOME OF THE BEST ADVENTURES HAPPEN INSIDE YOU.

When people talk about bucket lists, they often focus on doing things—climbing mountains, swimming with dolphins, or eating their weight in ice cream. But not every adventure involves checklists and physical activity. Some of the most meaningful items on your bucket list are about how you feel, connect, and grow.

This chapter is dedicated to those quieter adventures that don't make it onto Instagram but leave an imprint on your heart. So, grab your favorite comfy chair, take a deep breath, and dive into the Bucket List for the Soul.

Forgive Someone

(Forgiveness Isn't About Them....It's About Freeing Yourself)

Holding onto anger or resentment is like carrying a backpack full of bricks. Heavy, unnecessary, and bad for your posture. Forgiveness doesn't mean excusing someone's behavior. It just means you're ready to stop letting it **weigh you down**.

REALITY CHECK

Forgiving someone **doesn't mean** they have to be **in your life.** You might not get an **apology.** That's okay. It's a process, not a **one-time event.**

QUOTABLE

"I forgave someone last week. Then I saw them double-dip a chip at a party, and now we're back to square one."

NO...SERIOUSLY?

An **89-year feud** over a hat finally ended. Two families in Spain fought for almost a century over a stolen hat. In 2015, their great-grandkids finally forgave each other. Talk about holding a grudge.

Forgiveness stopped a war. In 1861, the U.S. accidentally invaded Canada due to a border mix-up. Canada forgave them immediately, proving that Canadians really are that nice.

SOUL CHALLENGE 1

Forgive someone. Write them a letter—whether you send it or not is up to you.
Bonus points if it's in the form of a poem or song.

Tell Someone You Love Them

(Life Is Short. Say It Out Loud)

We often assume people know how we feel about them. But here's the truth: **it's always worth saying**. It could be a romantic partner, a family member, or a friend who's been there through thick and thin, telling someone you love them is a bucket list item worth repeating.

REALITY CHECK

It might feel **awkward.** Do it anyway. They might cry. That's okay. You'll never **regret saying it**—but you might **regret not saying it.**

QUOTABLE

"I told my best friend I loved them. They said, 'Are you dying?' Honestly, fair question."

NO...SERIOUSLY?

A man once **sent 7,000 love letters**... and got rejected. The Hungarian man wrote to the same woman every day for 19 years. She finally married the mailman instead.

A man proposed over the radio... to the **wrong person**. He went on live radio to propose, but the host called the wrong woman. She said yes before realizing she wasn't the fiancée.

SOUL CHALLENGE 2

Call, text, or tell someone in person that **you love them**.
Be specific about why.
Bonus points if one or both of you have a little cry.

Perform a Random Act of Kindness

(Keep It Simple. The Smallest Acts Often Mean The Most)

Buy a coffee for a stranger. Leave an encouraging note on someone's car windshield. Donate to a local charity. Acts of kindness **aren't about grand gestures**. Tiny ripples of goodness spread farther than you'll ever see.

REALITY CHECK

You might never see the result of **your kindness**. That's the point. Sometimes, **people won't notice**. That's okay, too. **Kindness is contagious**.

QUOTABLE

"I stood outside the supermarket and handed out roses. Every smile warmed my heart."

NO...SERIOUSLY?

A guy helped a woman with a flat tire... and **married Her**. He stopped to help a stranger on the road, and years later, they were husband and wife. Who needs dating apps?

A woman paid for a **stranger's coffee**... and accidentally started a 3-hour chain reaction. She bought the person behind her a drink, then paid for the next person, and so on... for over 300 customers. The barista just wanted it to end.

> **SOUL CHALLENGE 3**
>
> Perform one **random act of kindness**. Don't overthink it—just do it.
> **Bonus points** if you make a person smile.

Apologize for Something You Regret

(A Genuine Apology Can Heal Old Wounds For Both Sides)

We've all said or done things we wish we could take back. Apologizing doesn't erase the past, but it can **soften its edges**. Whether it's a friend, a sibling, or even yourself, saying "I'm sorry" is an act of courage.

REALITY CHECK

The other person **might not accept it.** That's not your job to **control**. It might feel **awkward**. Don't stop. Even if nothing changes, you'll feel **lighter.**

QUOTABLE

"I apologized for something I did in high school. The person said they didn't remember it. Great. Now I'm embarrassed twice."

NO...SERIOUSLY?

A mayor apologized for something that happened 300 years ago. In 2008, the mayor of Boston formally **apologized for the Salem Witch Trials**.

A kid once mailed a **handwritten apology to NASA**. The 7-year-old boy stole a pen from NASA's gift shop. Feeling guilty, he returned it back with a note: "I'm sorry. Don't send me to space jail."

> ### SOUL CHALLENGE 4
>
> Think of one **apology** you owe. Write it, say it, or send it. Do your best.
> **Bonus points** if you give them a little gift, like flowers or chocolate.

Spend The Day Listening to Your Favorite Music

(Headphones Make Everything Sound Better)

Music can crack open even the most stubborn parts of our hearts. Spend a day revisiting old favorites, discovering new songs, and letting yourself **feel all the feelings**.

REALITY CHECK

You might **cry** at a song you haven't heard in years. You'll probably **sing off-key. Embrace it.** Nostalgia is a **powerful thing.**

QUOTABLE

"I made a playlist of my favorite songs. Halfway through, I realized I've been emotionally unstable since 1975."

NO...SERIOUSLY?

The world's longest playlist would take over 100 years to finish. A Spotify user created a **playlist with over 2 million songs**. If you start now, you might finish by 2125.

A Man once got banned from a café... for playing "**Bohemian Rhapsody**" 20 times in a row. The barista begged him to stop. He just said "So you think you can stop me and spit in me eye?"

SOUL CHALLENGE 5

Make a **playlist of songs** that make you feel something. Play it. Loudly.
Bonus points if you share it with a friend and they love it as much as you do.

Sometimes It's About Feeling, Not Doing

The most meaningful adventures don't always require tickets, passports, or hiking boots. Sometimes, they just require vulnerability, kindness, and a **little courage**.

So let yourself feel deeply, love loudly, and rest unapologetically. Because at the end of the day, the **adventures of the soul** are the ones that stay with you the longest.

Here's to the quiet moments, the big feelings, and the adventures in the spaces between adventures.

9

Oops! I Did it Again

When Things Go Hilariously Wrong.

Ah, the best-laid plans. You had a vision: a perfect hot air balloon ride, a stress-free cooking class, or a karaoke performance that would earn you a standing ovation. But life, dear friend, had other ideas.

This chapter is dedicated to those gloriously imperfect bucket list moments, where things went sideways, upside-down, or straight into chaos. But here's the thing: those "oops" moments? They often make the best stories.

So, let's celebrate the hiccups, the missteps, and the outright disasters that turned into memories you'll laugh about for years to come.

The Great Canoe Incident

(The Day The Canoe Won)

You had a vision: **gliding serenely across a glassy lake**, the sun setting in the background, maybe a gentle breeze tousling your hair. Instead, you ended up clinging to an overturned canoe, trying to rescue your waterlogged snack bag.

REALITY CHECK

Canoes are **not as stable** as they appear in movies. Wear **waterproof shoes**. Paddles have a way of disappearing when you need them most. And let's be clear—**snacks do not float**.

QUOTABLE

"I gracefully entered the canoe... by which I mean I fell in, and the canoe left without me."

NO...SERIOUSLY?

Some canoe marathon races have a **beer category**. You must chug a beer before paddling to the next checkpoint. That's one way to stay hydrated.

And in the 1800s, people **smuggled cattle in canoes** across rivers to avoid paying taxes. That's some serious farm-to-table dedication.

> ### OOPS CHALLENGE 1
>
> Retell the story with pride if you've ever had a **canoe or kayak mishap**.
> **Bonus points** if you include dramatic hand gestures.

Karaoke Disaster Night

(Pick a Song You Actually Know. The Chorus Isn't Enough)

The plan was simple: **grab the mic, sing your heart** out, and become a local karaoke legend. The reality? The lyrics vanished from your brain, the high notes betrayed you, and somewhere in the distance, a dog started howling.

REALITY CHECK

Microphones are **unforgiving** to nerves. Halfway through, you'll realize you've **forgotten every lyric**. The audience will cheer anyway—**out of kindness**.

QUOTABLE

"The karaoke machine froze during my song—probably out of self-preservation."

NO...SERIOUSLY?

The **inventor of karaoke** forgot to patent it. He made zero money from his genius idea. Ouch.

And did you know? **Karaoke means** "Empty Orchestra." In Japanese, "kara" means empty hand, "oke" is short for orchestra—so technically, you're just singing into the void.

OOPS CHALLENGE 2

Share your **karaoke mishap story**.
Bonus points if you make someone cry with laughter.

The Cooking Class Chaos

(The Recipe For Disaster)

 You signed up for a **cooking class**. You imagined yourself as a sophisticated chef, gracefully chopping vegetables and presenting a Michelin-star-worthy dish. What actually happened? Smoke alarms, lopsided soufflés, and sauce stains that might be permanent.

REALITY CHECK

Your casserole might look like a **crime against humanity**. **Recipes lie**. They do. And let's be honest, you might get bored and **start a food fight**.

QUOTABLE

"I tried a new recipe today. The smoke alarm was the only thing that was impressed."

NO...SERIOUSLY?

The **first cooking show** aired in 1946. It was called *Cookery* and had one camera, no editing, and a host who burned himself on live TV. Classic.

And did you know? There's an actual condition called **mageirocophobia**—the intense fear of cooking. These people must love takeout.

OOPS CHALLENGE 3

Share your **best cooking fail** story.
Bonus points if you managed to eat the disaster anyway.

Go Anywhere–Except Where You Planned

(Resistance is Futile. Go With The Flow)

You set off on a **spontaneous day trip**. The plan? Explore, have fun, and maybe find a charming little café. The reality? Wrong turns, closed attractions, and a suspicious gas station sandwich.

REALITY CHECK

GPS directions **can and will betray you**. "Open year-round" is apparently **up for interpretation**. And **gas station snacks** are their own **food group.**

QUOTABLE

"I planned a day trip to the beach. I ended up in a field full of cows. I made friends with the white one."

NO...SERIOUSLY?

Some airports have a **'Mystery Flight' option**. In Australia, you can buy a plane ticket without knowing where you're going—which is a great idea unless you hate surprises.

And the longest unplanned road trip **lasted over a year**. A couple left home in 1985 for a 'short drive' and didn't return until 1986.

OOPS CHALLENGE 4

Tell someone your **hilariously misguided travel story**. **Bonus points** if it involves penguins.

When 'Getting Fit' Turns into 'Getting Help'

(Stretching is Only a Suggestion)

You decided to **try something active**: yoga, Zumba, or a leisurely bike ride. You had visions of grace, flexibility, and maybe even a little smug satisfaction. Instead, you discovered that balance is a lie and yoga poses are not for the faint of hamstrings.

REALITY CHECK

Spandex hides nothing. Nothing. Gravity will absolutely have its say. And the best trick? Try exercising in the morning **before your brain figures out what you're doing**.

QUOTABLE

"I don't need a personal trainer as much as I need someone to follow me around and slap unhealthy foods out of my hand"

NO...SERIOUSLY?

Treadmills were invented as a punishment. In the 1800s, they were used in prisons—prisoners walked for hours to grind grain or pump water.

And did you know? **Exercise can make you taller**—temporarily. After sleeping and stretching, people gain up to half an inch in height—until gravity squashes them back down.

OOPS CHALLENGE 5

Share your **funniest fitness attempt.**
Bonus points if you still occasionally try it again.

The Memory Mishap

(I Came, I Saw, I Forgot)

We've all done it—walked into a room with **purpose**, only to immediately forget why we're there. It's the human equivalent of buffering.

REALITY CHECK

Whatever you're looking for, **it's probably in the fridge.** Your brain was **probably trying to save you** from doing something boring. And sometimes, you'll **never remember.** And that's okay**.**

QUOTABLE

"I walked into the kitchen with purpose… and walked out with a cookie instead. Mission unclear, but snack acquired."

NO…SERIOUSLY?

It's called the **"Doorway Effect."** Scientists found that walking through a doorway actually makes your brain "reset"—so, it's not just you.

And here's a fun trick, if you forget why you walked into a room, **walk backward out of it.** This helps reset your memory, but will also make you look a little crazy.

> **OOPS CHALLENGE 6**
>
> Next time you **forget why you entered a room,** shrug, laugh, and grab a snack**.**
> **Bonus Points** if you go backward through the door while making beeping sounds.

Laugh It Off, Move On, and Tell the Story

Not every bucket list moment is going to go perfectly. In fact, most of them won't. But that's the fun of it. The best stories aren't about flawless victories. They're about hilarious failures, happy accidents, and unexpected detours.

So embrace the chaos, laugh at the mess-ups, and remember: if nothing else, it's a good story for the next time you have an audience.

Here's to the blunders, the bloopers, and the belly laughs—because sometimes, the "oops" moments are the real bucket list gold.

10

Wild Card List

Rules are meant to be bent, broken, and occasionally ignored.

Welcome to the chapter where anything goes, well, almost anything. This is the place for the spontaneous, the slightly ridiculous, and the beautifully unplanned bucket list adventures. Think of this as the "miscellaneous" drawer of your life goals.

Want to dye your hair purple? Go for it. Ever dreamed of performing at an open mic night? The stage is yours. Want to start a flash mob in your living room? Please send me the video.

This chapter is about giving yourself permission to be silly, brave, and unapologetically YOU—because if not now, then when?

So grab your metaphorical (or literal) party hat because things are about to get delightfully unpredictable.

Perform on a Stage

(Or At Least in Front Of a Mirror)

It could be a karaoke night, an open mic comedy set, or a dramatic poetry reading. Standing in front of an audience can be both **terrifying and exhilarating**, but here's the secret: nobody cares if you mess up. They are just happy you showed up

REALITY CHECK

Nerves are just excitement in disguise. Someone will **record it**. That's cool. And you'll feel like a **rock star** afterward, even if it's just applause from your dog.

QUOTABLE

"I read my poem using jazz hands and dramatic pauses. A couple in the front row left traumatized."

NO...SERIOUSLY?

A Broadway actor once forgot his mic was on backstage... and the entire audience heard him using the bathroom. **The flush got the biggest applause of the night.**

And in a moment of ultimate relaxation, a man playing a "**dead body**" on stage was so comfortable he actually fell asleep. The cast had to kick him gently to wake him up for the curtain call.

WILD CARD CHALLENGE 1

Perform something—anything—in front of an audience. A song, a joke, a dramatic reading of your grocery list. Own the stage!
Bonus Points if you take a bow when you finish.

Adopt A Pet

(Start With Something Low-Maintenance, Like a Fish. Or a Cactus)

Pets bring joy, love, and the occasional hairball into our lives. Whether it's a dog, a cat, or a very judgmental goldfish, adopting or befriending an animal can add a little sparkle to your days.

REALITY CHECK

Pets come with responsibilities, like feeding, cleaning, and not accidentally teaching them **bad habits**. They'll become the boss of your home. And yes, you'll **love them unconditionally.**

QUOTABLE

"I adopted a cat. She owns the couch, the chair, and possibly my soul. It's fine; I'm fine."

NO...SERIOUSLY?

A small town in Alaska elected a **cat named Stubbs as mayor**. He held office for 20 years and never raised taxes.

And in the ultimate surprise adoption, a family in China took in what they thought was a large, fluffy dog. It took two years before they **realized it was a bear**.

WILD CARD CHALLENGE 2

Adopt a pet, volunteer at a shelter, or pet-sit for a friend. Animals are good for the soul.
Bonus points if you adopt a dog and name it "Bark Twain."

Crash a Party

(Bring Snacks. It's harder to Kick Out Someone Holding a Tray of Brownies)

There's something oddly thrilling about walking into a party where **nobody knows you** and just... blending in. And you may make a lifelong friend or at least get free cake out of the deal

REALITY CHECK

Confidence is key. **Fake it** if you have to. It's more fun if it's a community event or festival, not someone's wedding. And no matter what happens, you'll have an **outrageous story** afterward.

QUOTABLE

"I crashed a neighborhood barbecue. I didn't know anyone, but I left with three new friends and a Tupperware of potato salad!"

NO...SERIOUSLY?

A woman crashed a birthday party but got caught when she loudly **sang Happy Birthday... to the wrong person**.

A man **crashed a wedding reception**, thinking nobody would notice. The event was being broadcast live. His face was everywhere.

> **WILD CARD CHALLENGE 3**
>
> **Attend a party or event** where you don't know many people. Be brave, be friendly, and remember that free snacks are always worth it.
> **Bonus point**s if you give a speech.

Dye Your Hair a Wild Color

(Or Wear A Wig)

Why not? Purple, blue, neon green, **your hair is your canvas**, and life's too short for dull hair. If you've always played it safe, this is your moment to let your inner rainbow shine.

REALITY CHECK

You might end up **staining your sink**. If you have no hair, go for a **temporary tattoo**. Hair grows back. And **wigs** exist.

QUOTABLE

"I dyed my hair electric blue. My grandkids asked if I'm going away for a while like Uncle Frank."

NO...SERIOUSLY?

Ancient Romans used bird droppings to bleach their hair blonde. Good luck washing that out.

Special UV-reactive dyes exist, meaning your hair could **light up like a nightclub sign**. Perfect for late-night grocery shopping.

WILD CARD CHALLENGE 4

Dye your hair (or wear a wig) in a color that makes you feel fabulous. Take a selfie.
Bonus points for men if they dye their facial hair.

Create Your Own Wild Card List Item

(If it Feels Fun and Slightly Silly, You're On The Right Track)

This is your chance to think **outside the bucket list box**. What's one thing you've always wanted to do, no matter how random, small, or absurd it seems? Write it down. Then go do it.

REALITY CHECK

It **doesn't have to be original,** just fun. If it's really unique, you should probably **copyright it.** And as a general rule, **avoid using pointy things.** Pointy things lead to bleedy things.

QUOTABLE

"I joined a karaoke competition and did an interpretive dance instead of singing."

NO...SERIOUSLY?

A man wanted a **Chinese symbol for "strength"** but later found out it meant "toilet demon."

And sometimes, **starting a new hobby becomes a full-time job.** A woman tried knitting for fun and accidentally started a knitting business.

> ## WILD CARD CHALLENGE 5
>
> Create one **Wild Card bucket list activity** of your own and do it. Yes, even if it's ridiculous.
> **Bonus points** for any activity involving balloons.

The Best Items Are the Unexpected Ones

Sometimes, the most memorable adventures are the ones you didn't plan for. Singing karaoke in public, adopting a new pet, or dyeing your hair purple, are about letting go of expectations and **just enjoying life**.

So throw caution (and maybe a handful of confetti) to the wind, embrace your inner rebel, and remember: the best stories start with, 'Why not?'

11

Your Legacy

Stories Deserve to Outlive You.

Welcome to a chapter where we transition from adventure to legacy. A bucket list isn't solely about exciting experiences or amusing moments; it's also about the impact you leave on the world. What stories will people share about you? What lessons will they remember? What little pieces of you will endure after you're gone?

This chapter isn't about being somber or overly serious. It's about thinking intentionally about the gifts you can leave behind—whether they're stories, objects, wisdom, or traditions.

Because in the end, a life well-lived isn't just measured in what you did—it's measured in how you made others feel and what you passed along.

Let's build a legacy worth smiling about.

Write Down Your Life Lessons

(Keep it Simple. Write As if You're Talking to a Friend)

We all have lessons **we've learned the hard way**, wisdom we've gathered over the years, and things we wish we'd known sooner. Whether it's profound insights about love or lighthearted reminders like *"Never trust a fart after 60,"* your experiences have value.

REALITY CHECK

You don't have to write a novel. Even a **list** works. Some lessons will make you **laugh**. Others might make you cry. But rest assured—someone, someday, will **cherish** your words.

QUOTABLE

"You can't have your cake and eat it too, unless you bake two cakes."

NO...SERIOUSLY?

A 102-year-old man gave the best life lesson ever. When asked about his longevity secret, he said, "Eat what you want, do what you love, and avoid annoying people." Wise words, indeed.

And the **shortest life lesson** ever? A monk once summed up wisdom in just two words: "Let go." Simple, powerful, and possibly a great excuse to avoid cleaning the garage.

> ### LEGACY CHALLENGE 1
>
> Write down **five life lessons** you want to share. Start simple.
> **Bonus points** if one of the lessons is about dessert.

Leave a Video Message

(Speak From The Heart. Don't Over-Rehearse)

Imagine your great-grandkids **watching a video of you in 50 years**. What would you say? Would you tell a story? Share advice? Sing a song? Your future family deserves to know you—not just as a name in a family tree, but as a person with quirks, humor, and wisdom.

REALITY CHECK

You might feel **awkward talking to a camera.** Push through. You'll probably **ramble.** That's okay. Future generations will **love every second.**

QUOTABLE

"If you're watching this in the future and you have a time machine, please send me next week's lottery numbers."

NO...SERIOUSLY?

The **first-ever video message** was... a blink. In 1888, the first recorded video ever was just a man blinking. No deep thoughts, just "proof of eyeballs."

And did you know? **Astronauts sent the first video message** from space... and nobody knew how to respond. Ground control was so shocked that they forgot to reply for five minutes.

LEGACY CHALLENGE 2

Record a **short video message** for future generations.
Save it somewhere safe.
Bonus points for using a French accent.

Create Something Tangible

(It Doesn't Have to Be Perfect—it Just Has to Be You)

You may not be crafty, but creating something with your own hands carries a **certain magic**. A quilt made from old T-shirts, a scrapbook of your favorite memories, or even a series of handwritten letters becomes priceless keepsakes.

REALITY CHECK

It'll take time. Be **patient** with yourself. You might get glue everywhere**.** Or **glitter. Forever glitter.** And most importantly, someone will **cherish it long after you're gone.**

QUOTABLE

"This scrapbook has blood, sweat, and glitter in it. Mostly glitter."

NO...SERIOUSLY?

The first-ever DIY craft was... **a 100,000-year-old necklace**. Ancient humans made jewelry from snail shells, proving that people have always been obsessed with accessories.

The most expensive handmade item? Someone knitted a gold-threaded **sweater worth $250,000**. Great for looking rich, terrible for laundry day.

> **LEGACY CHALLENGE 3**
>
> **Start one tangible project.** A scrapbook, a quilt, or even a handwritten series of letters.
> **Bonus points** if you incorporate a touch of glitter, sequins, or something equally unnecessary.

Plant a Tree

(Or Something That Will Outlive You)

Planting something: A tree, a garden, or even a resilient little cactus will create a legacy that grows long after you've walked away. Trees, in particular, are incredible gifts. They grow, they shade, they outlast us.

REALITY CHECK

You might need to **water it... regularly**. You won't see it **grow fully**—but someone else will. It's a deeply **symbolic** act.

QUOTABLE

"I hope people remember me for the time I accidentally started a conga line at a funeral."

NO...SERIOUSLY?

Trees have a **secret underground network**. Scientists discovered that trees talk to each other through their roots, like a botanical social media.

An Indian man planted a tree daily, and now his forest is **bigger than Central Park**. Meanwhile, most of us forget to water a houseplant.

> ### LEGACY CHALLENGE 4
>
> **Plant something**—anything—that will outlast you.
> **Bonus points** if it survives the first month.

Your Story Deserves to Be Told

A legacy isn't about grand monuments or impressive resumes—it's about small, meaningful acts that ripple outward. It's about leaving behind something that says, *"I was here, and I cared."*

So whether it's a recipe, a story, a tree, or a simple "I love you," every little thing you pass along **becomes part of your legacy**.

Here's to a life well-lived, a legacy well-loved, and stories that last long after we've taken our final bow.

12

Have A Laugh

YOU ARE NOT DOING IT RIGHT IF YOU'RE NOT SNORTING WITH LAUGHTER AT LEAST ONCE.

Welcome to the chapter dedicated entirely to joy, silliness, and belly laughs—the kind that makes your face hurt and your stomach ache in the best way possible. Because let's face it: life is serious enough already. Your bucket list deserves a section devoted to sheer, unfiltered fun.

These aren't grand gestures or profound life lessons. These moments are designed to make you giggle, chortle, snicker, and (if lucky) let out one of those glorious, slightly embarrassing snorts.

So put on your silliest socks, embrace your inner goofball, and dip into a chapter where the only goal is to have a ridiculously good time.

Wear Something Ridiculous in Public

(Call It Trendsetting)

Ever wanted to **wear a feather boa to the grocery store?** Rock a tutu at the post office? Sport mismatched socks and a Hawaiian shirt just because you can? This is your sign to do it. Life's too short to save the funny hats for costume parties.

REALITY CHECK

You'll get some **strange looks**. Wave and smile. At least one person will **compliment your outfit**. Bask in it. And, surprisingly, you'll feel oddly... **free**.

QUOTABLE

"I call this outfit 'caught in a tornado at the thrift store."

NO...SERIOUSLY?

The world record for most clothes worn at once? A man in Canada put on **260 T-shirts** in layers, creating a fabric fortress of sweat.

In some cities, it's **illegal to wear a disguise in public**. In parts of the U.S., dressing up in costume outside of Halloween can technically get you fined. So, think twice before grocery shopping as Batman.

LAUGHTER CHALLENGE 1

Wear something **hilariously** over-the-top in public. **Bonus points** if you get a stranger to laugh.

Prank Call a Friend

(Keep it Light-Hearted. No Pretending to Be The IRS)

Prank calls aren't just for middle schoolers. They're for the young at heart. Call a friend and pretend you're a radio DJ offering them an imaginary prize. Or tell them you're a pizza delivery driver... and they didn't order pizza.

REALITY CHECK

They might **recognize your voice immediately.** Keep going. **Laughter** is pretty much guaranteed. And don't forget to say, **"Just kidding!"**

QUOTABLE

"I called my friend, pretending to be a customer service representative for their toaster. We had an earnest conversation about bread settings."

NO...SERIOUSLY?

Before Caller ID, some towns **banned prank calls** because people kept calling pizza places and ordering 50 pizzas for their enemies.

In 2008, pranksters tricked a billionaire into sending them **$15 million.** This is why banks now double-check everything.

LAUGHTER CHALLENGE 2

Prank call a friend in the kindest, most ridiculous way possible.
Bonus points if you can get them to say the word "Kangaroo".

Talk to an Animal Like Best Friends

(Ducks Are Particularly Good Listeners)

Maybe a squirrel in the park, a neighbor's cat, or a particularly judgmental pigeon have a **full-on conversation with an animal**. Ask them about their day. Share your hopes and dreams. Wait patiently for their response.

REALITY CHECK

Animals are **terrible conversationalists.** Passersby might give you **side-eye.** Ignore them. But surprisingly, you'll feel **oddly better afterward.**

QUOTABLE

"I had a deep conversation with a goat today. He seemed uninterested, but I think we connected on some level."

NO...SERIOUSLY?

Some animals can actually **recognize human words**. Dogs understand about 165 words, while some parrots can learn over 1,000. So, yes—your pet might actually be judging you.

A parrot once testified in court. A pet parrot kept repeating suspicious phrases from a crime scene… and helped convict a murderer.

LAUGHTER CHALLENGE 3

Talk to an animal for at least five minutes.
Bonus points if you make a friend in the process.

People-Watch and Invent Backstories

(The Best Free Show in Town)

Sit somewhere public, watch the people around you, and **invent completely ridiculous backstories** for them. Is that guy in the blue shirt an undercover superhero? Is that woman in the corner secretly writing the next bestselling romance novel?

REALITY CHECK

Your **imagination will run wild.** Let it. You'll probably start **laughing** at inappropriate times. And you'll feel like a **budget Sherlock Holmes.**

QUOTABLE

"That guy with the fedora? Definitely, a retired pirate turned smoothie enthusiast."

NO...SERIOUSLY?

There's a **professional people-watching event**. In some cities, there are official "people-watching competitions." The goal? Create the most ridiculous backstory for strangers.

In 2014, a couple watched a guy in a coffee shop pretend to be on an important phone call—but his phone screen was clearly locked the whole time. They gave him a **standing ovation** when he finished.

LAUGHTER CHALLENGE 4

Spend 30 minutes **people-watching** and invent at least five hilarious backstories.
Bonus points if a llama is in one of the stories.

Laughter Belongs in Every Bucket List

If there's one thing worth adding to every bucket list, it's laughter. The kind that makes you snort, cry, and clutch your stomach because you can't breathe.

Wearing silly socks, dancing badly, or talking to ducks, let yourself lean into the ridiculous. Life is better when you're laughing—especially when you're laughing at yourself.

Here's to silliness, snorts, and stories that make you **smile whenever you tell them**.

13

Grandkids and Giggles

"Fun Grandparent" is the best title you can earn

Grandkids are a bit like time machines. They remind you what it's like to see the world with fresh eyes, ask endless "why" questions, and find joy in the simplest things, like bubbles, stickers, or spaghetti noodles are hilariously floppy.

This chapter is dedicated to grand adventures with your grandkids—the memories they'll carry forever. Whether you're building pillow forts, baking cookies, or sharing a story from your childhood, these moments aren't just fun—they're legacy-building magic.

So, grab your superhero cape (you know you have one), put on your comfiest sneakers, and let's make some memories that will have your grandkids saying, *"My grandparent is the coolest person I know."*

Bake Something Delicious

(Embrace The Mess. The Flour Isn't Going Back in The Bag Once it's Out)

Baking with grandkids isn't about precision. It's about creating edible chaos. Cupcakes, cookies, or even just "creative toast"—the goal is to have fun, taste-test liberally, and ignore the kitchen disaster you'll have to clean up later.

REALITY CHECK

Flour will end up in places you **didn't know flour could go.** Half the chocolate chips will **mysteriously disappear.** And the final product might **look questionable… but it'll taste amazing.**

QUOTABLE

"We baked cookies together. The kitchen looks like a flour tornado hit it. Still we have six semi-edible cookies and a dozen happy memories."

NO...SERIOUSLY?

A grandma once mixed up **sugar and salt**... and created "Disaster Cookies." The grandkids still ate them out of loyalty. One gagged. The dog refused them.

Cookies were invented by accident. Bakers used to test oven temperatures by baking small bits of dough—and accidentally invented cookies. Best mistake ever.

> ### GRANDKIDS CHALLENGE 1
>
> **Bake something** simple and fun with your grandkids. **Bonus points** for colorful frosting and sprinkles.

Do an Arts and Crafts Extravaganza

(Cover Your Furniture. Cover Your Carpet. Cover Everything)

Art projects are a **gateway to creativity, laughter**, and a small chance of glue-related incidents. Grab some paper, markers, glue, and whatever random craft supplies you can find, and let creativity run wild.

REALITY CHECK

Glitter is **forever.** Accept it. Someone will **eat a crayon.** The final art piece **might not make sense,** but it'll be **yours.**

QUOTABLE

"Art & Crafts time with the grandkids is just a race to see who gets stuck to the table first."

NO...SERIOUSLY?

Crayons were invented to **stop kids from eating chalk**. In the early 1900s, kids kept munching on school chalk—so *Crayola* invented non-toxic, colorful crayons to distract them.

Glitter is forever. Scientists discovered that glitter is practically impossible to get rid of. If you spill it once, your house will sparkle for eternity.

GRANDKIDS CHALLENGE 2

Have a craft day. Display the finished art as if it were in the Louvre.
Bonus points if the kids glitter bomb the cat.

Grandkids + Board Games = Laughs

(Let Them Win... Sometimes)

Board games are a timeless bonding activity. It could be Candy Land, Monopoly, or something with a thousand tiny game pieces. The key is to laugh, play fair (mostly), and celebrate every silly victory.

REALITY CHECK

Someone will **invent their own rules.** Monopoly may **test family bonds. Victory dances** are encouraged.

QUOTABLE

"We started with Scrabble, but now it's a heated debate over whether 'fartzilla' is a word."

NO...SERIOUSLY?

Grandkids play to win. A study found that **kids secretly cheat** at board games more than adults. Watch out for suspicious rule changes!

The **longest** Monopoly game lasted 70 days.

> ### GRANDKIDS CHALLENGE 3
>
> **Have a board game day.** Keep score, play fair, and let the winner choose the victory dance.
> **Bonus points** if the victory dance includes glitter.

Go on a Nature Adventure

(Even if it's Just The Backyard)

You don't need to hike up a mountain to have a nature adventure. A walk in the park, a backyard scavenger hunt, or even cloud-watching on a picnic blanket can turn into an **unforgettable day**.

REALITY CHECK

Bugs will be **discussed at length.** Someone will collect **"treasures" (a.k.a. rocks and sticks).** You might end up with **grass stains.**

QUOTABLE

"We went on a nature walk. I identified a tree, a squirrel, and what might have been a very angry goose."

NO...SERIOUSLY?

A kid once collected "Cool Rocks" and accidentally **brought home a fossil**. He thought it was a weird rock, but a scientist later confirmed it was a 100-million-year-old fossil.

One national park had to put up a sign that said, "**Don't Push Your Friends Into the Geysers**." Apparently, some people need to be told not to shove Grandpa into Old Faithful.

GRANDKIDS CHALLENGE 4

Plan a backyard or park adventure. Create a scavenger hunt list and let curiosity lead the way.
Bonus points if the kids bring you a frog.

Write a Time Capsule Letter Together

(Seal It and Hide It Somewhere Special)

Write letters to your future selves together. Include silly predictions, draw doodles, and seal them in an envelope. Hide them in a drawer or bury them in a small time capsule. Promise to open them together in five or ten years.

REALITY CHECK

Their **predictions will be hilarious.** Your handwriting might get **critiqued.** And the letters will become **treasures over time.**

QUOTABLE

"Our time capsule letter is mostly advice like 'Don't trust anyone who doesn't like pizza.'"

NO...SERIOUSLY?

Some time capsules have been lost forever. The 1964 World's Fair buried a time capsule—but **forgot where**. It's still missing.

The world's oldest time capsule was buried in **1795**... and nobody knew what to do with it. When they found it, historians argued for weeks over whether they should open it or leave it sealed.

GRANDKIDS CHALLENGE 5

Write and seal time capsule letters. Pick a date to open them together.
Bonus points for remembering where you put the letters.

Ride a Carousel Together

(Beware The Green Horses. They Bite)

There's something magical about a carousel—the music, the lights, the brightly painted horses that somehow look both majestic and slightly haunted. Ride one together. Wave dramatically to strangers as you pass.

REALITY CHECK

You will **100% get dizzy.** Someone will take an **unflattering photo** of you mid-spin. And it's **impossible not to smile.**

QUOTABLE

"I picked the golden horse. His name was Sir Gallopington, and we're best friends now."

NO...SERIOUSLY?

The first carousels were actually **war training machines**. Medieval knights used them to practice jousting—so technically, your grandkids are training for battle.

A Grandma once rode a carousel for **8 hours straight**. She refused to get off until she set the record for most carousel rides in a day. Absolute legend.

> ## GRANDKIDS CHALLENGE 6
>
> **Find a carousel**, pick the most flamboyant horse, and ride it with childlike glee with your grandkids.
> **Bonus points** if you yell, "Ride 'em, Cowboy!"

Memories Are the Best Souvenirs

Grand adventures with grandkids are about connection, laughter, and creating stories they'll carry forever.

So bake the cookies, build the forts, tell the stories, and never underestimate the power of a silly dance party. Because to your grandkids, you're not just a grandparent—you're the architect of **unforgettable moments**.

Here's to shared laughter, sticky hands, and memories that will outlive the glitter and the cookie crumbs.

14

The Anti-Bucket List

Nope...Not Doing That.

Congratulations! You've made it through your bucket list—climbed metaphorical mountains, tackled puzzles, danced like nobody was watching, and maybe even wore socks with sandals (a bold move, truly). But let's face it: not everything belongs on your bucket list.

This chapter is dedicated to the *"Nope, absolutely not, never gonna happen"* side of life. Because just as it's important to say yes to adventures, it's equally valid—and hilarious—to say no to the things that make you shudder, cringe, or start googling, *"Is this safe for seniors?"*

So, sit back, relax, and let's celebrate the things you're perfectly happy not doing.

Skydiving

(Chutes Open 99.99% of The Time. Gravity is 100%. Do The Math)

Ah, skydiving. The classic bucket list item for thrill-seekers and people with **questionable decision-making skills**. Jumping out of a perfectly good airplane just to trust a backpack full of nylon isn't for everyone. And that's okay!

REALITY CHECK

There's an **alarming amount of paperwork** involved. You'll spend more time **signing waivers** than actually falling. And there's **no graceful way to land.**.

QUOTABLE

"I'm already fighting gravity daily—no need to give it extra opportunities."

NO...SERIOUSLY?

A guy skydived **without a parachute**... and survived. In 2016, a stuntman jumped from 25,000 feet without a parachute and landed in a net the size of a small backyard.

The oldest skydiver was **103 years old**. A great-grandma jumped out of a plane to celebrate her birthday. Her secret? "Just don't look down."

> ### ANTI-BUCKET LIST ACTIVITY 1
>
> Take a **virtual skydiving tour** on YouTube. Cheerfully remind yourself, "Nope, still not doing it."
> **Bonus points** if you spreadeagle on the couch and pretend you're really skydiving.

Swimming with Sharks

(Only Do it With Swimmers Slower Than You)

Some people think swimming with sharks is *"thrilling."* Others think it's ***"a terrible life choice."*** If you belong to the second group, congratulations; you value your limbs.

REALITY CHECK

You'll spend half the time convincing yourself that the cage is secure**.** Sharks **don't care** about your bucket list. They **care**

about lunch. And whatever you do, **don't watch Jaws the night before.**

QUOTABLE

"I figured if I wanted to be part of the food chain, I'd go to a buffet, not the ocean."

NO...SERIOUSLY?

Sharks don't actually **like the taste of humans**. Most attacks happen by accident. Scientists say humans are too bony and bland—which is either comforting or insulting.

A man got bitten by a shark... then **bit It back**. In 2007, a surfer fought back against a shark by biting its fin. The shark let go out of pure confusion.

ANTI-BUCKET LIST ACTIVITY 2

Watch a shark documentary. Enjoy the experience without risking becoming part of the food chain.
Bonus points if you hum the theme from the "Jaws" movie.

Learning to Surf

(10% Balance, 90% Getting Back on The Board)

Surfing looks cool in movies. The sun, the waves, the perfect tan. Reality? You'll spend most of the time falling off the board and wondering if seawater can permanently live in your nose.

REALITY CHECK

Balance is... **tricky.** The **ocean is very salty.** You'll discover this up close. And you'll never trust the phrase **"It's just a little wave"** again.

QUOTABLE

"I tried surfing once. I became one with the ocean. Mostly because I couldn't get back on the board."

NO...SERIOUSLY?

A **dog once won a surfing competition**. Yes, there is a world championship for surfing dogs. And yes, they probably surf better than most beginners.

A guy accidentally **surfed into a wedding**. He wiped out, got dragged to shore by a wave, and landed right in the middle of a beachfront wedding ceremony. The couple invited him to the reception.

ANTI-BUCKET LIST ACTIVITY 3

Watch surfing competitions on TV. Cheer for the professionals while lounging comfortably on your couch. **Bonus points** if you "hang ten" while grabbing another snack from the kitchen.

Camping in the Wilderness

(Where You're One Step Away From Becoming Bear Food)

Camping enthusiasts say it's about *"**connecting with nature.**"* You say it's about *"sleeping on rocks and being eaten alive by mosquitoes."* Guess what? You're both right.

REALITY CHECK

Tents are just **fabric excuses for a real roof.** Nature is **loud at night.** Like, really loud. And your **air mattress will absolutely deflate** at 2 AM.

QUOTABLE

"I tried camping once. I spent the night staring at a spider the size of a small car and reevaluating my choices."

NO...SERIOUSLY?

Some campers bring TVs. A study found that 20% of people bring televisions on camping trips. Nothing says "wilderness adventure" like binge-watching Netflix in a tent.

A camper thought **he heard a bear**... but it was just a snoring friend. He panicked, grabbed a stick, and tried to "scare" the bear—only to smack his best friend awake.

ANTI-BUCKET LIST ACTIVITY 4

Set up a **camping experience indoors**. Roast marshmallows over the stove. No mosquitoes allowed.
Bonus points if you dramatically point off into the distance and scream, "BIGFOOT!"

Bungee Jumping

(Go Down Screaming, Come Up Screaming. Repeat)

Leaping off a bridge with only a cord to catch you? Some call it exhilarating; others call it a quick way to **test their heart medication**.

REALITY CHECK

The **free fall** is shorter than the time you'll spend convincing yourself to jump. The ground **rushes up to meet you,** then says, **"Just kidding!"** And your **vocal cords will get a workout.**

QUOTABLE

"I stood on the edge for 5 minutes negotiating with my sanity. The got tired of waiting and pushed me off"

NO...SERIOUSLY?

The oldest bungee jumper was **96**. A great-grandpa jumped off a bridge just to prove he still had it.

A woman's **bungee cord snapped**... and survived. She fell into a river and swam to shore, proving that sometimes, luck is real

---

ANTI-BUCKET LIST ACTIVITY 5

Watch bungee jumping videos from the comfort of your couch. Marvel at the bravery (or insanity) of others. **Bonus points** for screaming like banshee each time they jump.

Running a Marathon

(26.2 Miles of Pain and Suffering)

Marathons are a testament to **human endurance** and the human ability to forget the comfort of sitting.

REALITY CHECK

Blisters become your **new companions.**
The **"runner's high"** is often just exhaustion in disguise. And porta-potties are the **unsung heroes.**

QUOTABLE

"I told the organizers I need a Porta-Potty, Snack Station, Chiropractor and Cardiologist every 500 yards. I didn't hear back from them."

NO...SERIOUSLY?

A guy once took a **taxi in the middle of a marathon**... and still won. He got caught when officials realized his shoes were too clean.

A man ran a **marathon while juggling**. He juggled three balls for the entire 26 miles—and only dropped them twice.

> **ANTI-BUCKET LIST ACTIVITY 6**
>
> Participate in a **charity walk**. Enjoy a leisurely pace, good company, and a worthy cause.
> **Bonus points** for detouring to a donut shop.

Doing Anything Involving Snakes

(We're Opting Out if it is Hisses, Slithers, or Has Fangs)

Snakes. That's it. That's the argument.

REALITY CHECK

Nope. Nope. Also, **Nope**.

QUOTABLE

"I once saw a huge snake on TV. It was devouring a pig. Snakes are scary."

NO…SERIOUSLY?

Snakes can **survive being frozen**. Some snakes can freeze solid in the winter and come back to life in the spring. Zombies? They are Zombie snakes.

A family kept finding socks in odd places—turns out a **snake was stealing them**. They discovered a ball python had been sneaking into their laundry room and collecting socks in a hidden corner.

> ### ANTI-BUCKET LIST ACTIVITY 7
>
> Watch **Snakes on a Plane** from the safety of your snake-free couch.
> **Bonus points** for giving a name to each snake.

It's Okay to Say No

Your bucket list isn't about ticking off every stereotypical "thrill-seeker" activity. It's about what brings YOU joy, laughter, and memories worth cherishing.

So skip the skydiving, dodge the sharks, and keep your feet firmly on solid ground. There's absolutely no shame in declaring, *"Nope, not today, adrenaline. I'm good."*

Adventure is personal, and your anti-bucket list is just as valid as your bucket list.

Now go pour yourself a drink, sit back in your favorite chair, and celebrate all the things you did do—and **all the things you wisely avoided.**

Dear Reader,

Congratulations! You've made it through Hold My Cane!—which means you either laughed your way to the finish line or are currently recovering from a giggle-induced injury (don't worry, we won't tell your doctor). Either way, we at *Plonker Publishing* have a tiny favor to ask—could you leave us a review?

It'll only take a minute or two, we promise! That's less time than it takes to find your reading glasses, wonder why you walked into the room, or get your grandkids to explain what a "QR code" is.

Just scan the QR code or click the universal link to share your thoughts! Your review helps other readers find this book and keeps our publisher from panic-eating all the office snacks. Thanks for reading—and for keeping life hilariously unpredictable!

https://mybook.to/NA5ODh5

Sincerely,

The Slightly Unhinged Team at Plonker Publishing

15

Reflections on a Bucket Well-Listed

Every Bucket List item is a Story.

Well, look at you! You've laughed, you've cried, and you've danced—probably not all at once, but hey, we're not here to judge. You've dipped your toes in oceans, solved puzzles, dyed your hair in colors that can only be described as "courageous," and maybe eaten cheesecake before dinner. In short, you've lived your best (and possibly most questionable) life.

This chapter is all about taking a step back, giving yourself a well-deserved high-five, and celebrating all the weird, wonderful, and slightly ridiculous moments you've had. It's about recognizing that every ticked-off box and every "I did it!" moment is a tiny trophy sitting on your life's mantelpiece—next to the "World's Best Procrastinator" mug.

So, let's take a breath, sit back, and soak it all in. Your bucket list might be a bit ragged around the edges, but hey—so is your spirit, and it's looking fabulous.

Look Back at Your Accomplishments

(Celebrate The Big AND Small Wins. Both Deserve Cake. And Cookies)

Take a deep breath and flip back through these pages (or your own personal bucket list journal). Every checked-off item is a little story, a memory, a snapshot of you deciding, "Yes, I'm doing this."

REFLECTION PROMPTS

Which item made you laugh the most? (Be honest—was it karaoke?)

Which one surprised you? (Don't just say "doing the worm" at that wedding.)

Which one was harder than you expected? (Like, how hard is it to make a souffle without a YouTube tutorial?)

NEW LIFESTYLE GOAL

"Looking back, I'm pretty proud of eating dessert before dinner. Honestly, I might make it a lifestyle."

> ### REFLECTION ACTIVITY 1
>
> Write down your **favorite bucket list moment** so far. Describe it, laugh about it, and—if you're feeling brave—share it with someone.

Share Your Stories

(Everyone Loves a Good Story. Not The One Involving The Police)

Your stories are treasures, and sharing them is like passing along little nuggets of joy, wisdom, and comedic gold. Whether it's over a cup of coffee, in a family group chat, or written down in a journal, your adventures deserve an audience.

REALITY CHECK

You might repeat the same story more than once. That's okay.

Not every detail needs to be shared (looking at you, karaoke night).

Someone will say, "Wait, you actually did that??"

DJ GRANDPA

"I told my family about my spontaneous dance party. Now they call me 'DJ Shufflin' Grandpa.' I might start my own YouTube Channel"

> ### REFLECTION ACTIVITY 2
> **Share one of your bucket list stories** with a friend, family member, or even a stranger at the grocery store.

Think About What's Next

(But Don't Overthink It)

Is your bucket list complete? Absolutely not. Buckets are meant to be refilled—like an all-you-can-eat buffet where you can always go back for more mashed potatoes. There's always a new sunset to chase, a story to tell, or a new way to embarrass yourself in public.

REFLECTION PROMPTS

What's one thing you didn't get to do (yet)?

What's one spontaneous adventure you could try next week?

What's something small but meaningful you could add to your list?

UNFINISHED BUSINESS

"My next bucket list item? Finish my bucket list. It's getting out of hand."

REFLECTION ACTIVITY 3

Write down one **new bucket list item**. Big, small, or utterly ridiculous—it doesn't matter. Just one.

Celebrate Yourself

(Balloons Are Optional, But Highly Recommended. Especially Blue Ones)

Completing even one bucket list item is a victory. Completing a dozen? That's a parade-worthy achievement. Take a moment to celebrate yourself. You've tried new things, stepped outside your comfort zone, and most importantly, you've had fun.

REFLECTION IDEAS

Have a little "Bucket List Celebration Night." Cake is mandatory.

Write yourself a congratulatory note. Make it overly flattering.

Toast to yourself with whatever beverage makes you feel like royalty (even if it's just coffee).

LIVING MY BEST LIFE

"Here's to Me. Explorer, Adventurer, Nap Enthusiast, and Occasional Snack Hoarder. Cheers!"

REFLECTION ACTIVITY 4

Celebrate in your own way—big or small. Just make sure it feels like you.

Pass the Bucket

(Not A Real Bucket)

Your bucket list isn't just about you—it's about the ripple effect. Share your stories, encourage your friends, and remind people that adventures don't have to be grand or expensive—they just have to be *yours*.

IDEAS FOR SHARING

Inspire someone else to start their own bucket list.

Gift this book to a friend who needs a nudge (and maybe some cookies).

Plan a bucket list day with your family and see who can eat the most tacos in one sitting.

PRIORITIZING NAPS

"I told my friend to start a bucket list. She said, 'Does sleeping in, count?' Yes. Yes, it does."

REFLECTION ACTIVITY 5

Encourage one person to start their own bucket list.
Share your favorite tip from this book.

Final Reflections

(The Bucket Is Never Empty)

Here's the secret about bucket lists: They're not about crossing off every single item. They're about laughing, trying, failing, succeeding, and making memories that stay with you forever.

It's not about the checkmarks—it's about the moments in between. The spontaneous laughter, the badly executed dance moves, and the satisfaction of trying something new (even if it involved a rubber chicken).

So, keep adding, keep checking, and most importantly, keep living. Because whether your next adventure is big, small, or somewhere in between, your bucket is already overflowing with amazing stories.

> ### FINAL TIP
>
> If it doesn't bring you **joy, excitement**, or at least a **good laugh**—it doesn't belong on your list.

www.ingramcontent.com/pod-product-compliance
Lightning Source LLC
Chambersburg PA
CBHW052144070526
44585CB00017B/1966